MONSTERS

Basilisks

By Lori Mortensen

KIDHAVEN PRESS
An imprint of Thomson Gale, a part of The Thomson Corporation

Detroit • New York • San Francisco • San Diego • New Haven, Conn.
Waterville, Maine • London • Munich

© 2006 Thomson Gale, a part of The Thomson Corporation.

Thomson and Star Logo are trademarks and Gale and KidHaven Press are registered trademarks used herein under license.

For more information, contact
KidHaven Press
27500 Drake Rd.
Farmington Hills, MI 48331-3535
Or you can visit our Internet site at http://www.gale.com

ALL RIGHTS RESERVED.
No part of this work covered by the copyright hereon may be reproduced or used in any form or by any means—graphic, electronic, or mechanical, including photocopying, recording, taping, Web distribution or information storage retrieval systems—without the written permission of the publisher.

Every effort has been made to trace the owners of copyrighted material.

PICTURE CREDITS: Cover image: Erich Lessing/Art Resource
ABC/Photofest, 33
akg-images/Cameraphoto, 14-15
akg-images/Elizabeth Disney, 30
Bridgeman Art Library, 12
British Library, 6
Cameraphoto/Art Resource, NY, 25
Charles Walker/Topfoto/The Image Works, 22
Corbis Sygma, 34
Erich Lessing/Art Resource, NY, 5
Fortean Picture Library, 21, 23
HIP/Art Resource, NY, 27
Jeffrey L. Rotman/CORBIS, 10
Photofest, 38
The Art Archive/Biblioteca Nazionale Marciana Venice/Dagli Orti, 18
Tim Flach/Stone, 9
Time Life Pictures/Getty Images, 37

LIBRARY OF CONGRESS CATALOGING-IN-PUBLICATION DATA

Mortensen, Lori, 1955–
　Basilisks / by Lori Mortensen.
　　p. cm. — (Monsters)
　Includes bibliographical references (p.　) and index.
　ISBN 0-7377-3529-5 (hard cover : alk. paper) 1. Basilisks (Mythical animals) I. Title.
II. Monsters (KidHaven Press)
　GR830.B3M67 2006
　398'.469—dc22

2006000748

Printed in China

Contents

Chapter 1
Attack of the Basilisk   4

Chapter 2
The Legendary Basilisk   17

Chapter 3
The Basilisk Strikes Again   29

Notes   40
Glossary   41
For Further Exploration   43
Index   45
About the Author   48

Chapter 1

Attack of the Basilisk

In 1999 author J.K. Rowling brought the deadliest **mythical** monster, the basilisk, back to life in her book *Harry Potter and the Chamber of Secrets*. In Harry's world, this monster is a gigantic poisonous snake that slithers through underground pipes at Hogwarts School of Witchcraft and Wizardry. The snake has fiery red eyes and long, sharp fangs. Readers could not wait to unravel the mystery of this evil snake and find out whether Harry would defeat it.

Harry Potter was not the first person, fictional or real, who feared the poisonous basilisk. Stories about this monstrous creature terrified people from biblical times through the **Middle Ages** and into the 16th century.

Monster Most "Fowl"

According to these stories, basilisks hatched from the eggs of seven-year-old roosters. Roosters laid eggs in the hottest month of summer or under the

A piper rides on the back of a fearsome basilisk.

Attack of the Basilisk

full moon. (No one ever explained *how* roosters laid eggs!) Basilisk eggs did not have ordinary shells. Instead, the eggs were covered with a tough, leathery skin that was yellow or lumpy. After the egg was laid, a toad, snake, or rooster sat on it for nine years while a basilisk slowly developed inside.

When the egg finally hatched, a monster emerged. It had the head, wings, and legs of a rooster and the body of a snake. The basilisk's red, black, and yellow colors warned of its deadly nature, just as wasps' and bees' colors do. The crea-

A man falls paralyzed after looking into the eyes of a basilisk.

ture was so powerful that some people believed it wore a crown on its head as a symbol of its strength. In France, legend said that basilisks had a single jeweled eye. Any person who could steal the eye would become rich, but those who tried and failed would go insane. Not everyone agreed on the number of legs basilisks had. Some people said basilisks crept on two legs, while others claimed they had four or eight.

People disagreed over how the basilisk killed, too. Some thought its bite caused victims to become rabid and die from **convulsions**. Others believed the stare from a basilisk's piercing red eyes was fatal. Some thought the basilisk destroyed with its fiery breath. And many believed the basilisk was so dreadful that anyone who looked at it became **petrified**.

However basilisks claimed their victims, the creatures were thought to be extremely poisonous. Wherever a basilisk went, it left venom so deadly it could turn lush land into a desert. As the venom spread, rocks exploded, bushes burned, and birds flying overhead dropped from the sky.

Death to the Basilisk

Besides being very poisonous, the basilisk was quite difficult to kill. Only three things could kill it. One was a weasel, the sole animal immune to the basilisk's powerful venom. If the weasel was bitten in the fight, it renewed its strength by eating rue, a

Attack of the Basilisk

bitter plant the basilisk's venom could not destroy. The crow of a rooster would also kill a basilisk. Upon hearing this sound, the monster would go into convulsions and die. Since no one knew when a basilisk might attack, many people during **medieval** times carried roosters or weasels with them in cages while they traveled.

The most popular way of killing a basilisk was to use a mirror. The brave challenger would carry a mirror or wear a suit of mirrors. When the basilisk saw its reflection, it died from fear at its own horrible appearance. This method was not perfect, however. Stories spread of how basilisk hunters perished because they forgot to keep their eyes closed when they attacked.

If a person did succeed in killing a basilisk, it was believed that hanging its carcass in a home or temple would keep spiders and swallows away. Burning the basilisk's dead body and rubbing its ashes on silver was thought to make silver look like gold.

Basileus

Although beliefs like these about basilisks were common, no one knows for certain how stories of the basilisk began. One clue is found in the word basilisk itself, which comes from the Greek word *basileus,* meaning "king." Experts suspect that basilisk stories arose when ancient Greek sailors and Roman conquerors returned from Africa and

The real-life cobra inspired stories of the mythical, snakelike basilisk.

Attack of the Basilisk

A mongoose devours a king cobra after biting off its head.

India with tales about real poisonous snakes they had seen. These snakes may have been cobras.

Certainly, some cobras would have looked kinglike. The Egyptian cobra, a deadly snake, has white markings on its head that look like a crown. Unlike other snakes, the cobra is able to move with its head held upright. As they saw the cobra's body rise up from its middle, travelers might have imagined it looked like a king ruling over other snakes. And one species, the king cobra, seems to hold itself above others, since it survives almost entirely by eating other snakes.

Other cobra behaviors might have helped give rise to stories about the basilisk as well. The spitting cobra defends itself by squirting a blinding spray of venom into an enemy's eyes. This may have led to the idea that basilisks could kill an enemy with a penetrating stare.

Mongoose Attack

Even the basilisk's fabled foe, the weasel, was probably based on the mongoose, the cobra's fiercest enemy. About the size of a weasel, the mongoose begins its attack by trying to get the snake to strike. Each time the cobra strikes, the mongoose darts out of the way. The cobra strikes again and again. Finally, when the cobra is exhausted, the mongoose attacks the snake, biting its head with its powerful jaws. Just like the weasel in the basilisk legend, the mongoose is nearly immune to the cobra's venom.

Whatever their origins, little by little stories about the basilisk spread. As the tales were repeated and exaggerated over time, details about the creature changed. By the 1st century A.D., people still believed the basilisk looked like a snake, but it had become so powerful, it was said to kill everything it encountered with its eyes, breath, or venom.

As people's fear increased, they began seeing evidence of the monster everywhere. If someone's

Pliny the Elder included a description of basilisks in his multi-volume encyclopedia.

cellar stank, people feared a basilisk lived there. If water became polluted, people believed a basilisk must be nearby. If someone died mysteriously, a basilisk was to blame.

Dreadful Monster

One of the most important sources of information about basilisks comes from a Roman named Pliny the Elder, who lived during the 1st century A.D. Determined to write down what he called "all the contents of the entire world,"[1] Pliny included a description of the basilisk in his 37-volume encyclopedia *Historia Naturalis,* written in A.D. 77.

Pliny filled his encyclopedia with commonly held beliefs and information from hundreds of Greek and Roman sources. When the other written sources were lost, Pliny's record became one of the earliest descriptions of the basilisk. Calling it a "dreadful monster," Pliny wrote, "It destroys all shrubs, not only by its contact, but those that it has breathed upon; it burns up all the grass too, and breaks the stones, so tremendous is its noxious [poisonous] influence. It was formerly a general belief that if a man on horseback killed one of these animals with a spear, the poison would run up the weapon and kill, not only the rider, but the horse as well."[2]

By the 13th century A.D. people had more reason to fear basilisks when sailors began selling **Jenny Hanivers**. These were fake monsters made from the dried remains of skates, rays, and mantas. Fishermen probably got the idea because of the ray's humanlike face. With a little cutting, tying, and folding, fishermen turned flat fish into basilisks, mermaids, and dragons. Fishermen gave basilisk Jenny Hanivers the body and wings of a bird and the tail of a snake. It did not take long for the fishermen to realize that selling the fake monsters to

A sixteenth-century painting portrays efforts by a saint to rid a princess of the demon basilisk that controls her.

ignorant **landlubbers** was an easy way to make money.

Nobody knows why the fake monsters were called Jenny Hanivers. Some experts believe the name might have come from *anvers,* the French word for Antwerp, a busy seaport in Belgium where fishermen sold Jenny Hanivers. Others believe it might have been the name of a fisherman's sweetheart.

Basilisks

Books of Beasts

As people bought the fake monsters, more stories about basilisks spread. The legend of the basilisk became so familiar that basilisks were included in animal stories written by European monks during the Middle Ages to teach Christian morals and lessons. Eventually, these stories were collected into popular books called **bestiaries**, meaning "books of beasts." In some bestiaries, the basilisk represented the devil because it looked like a snake, and in the *Bible*, the devil appears to Eve in

Attack of the Basilisk

the form of a snake. In other bestiaries, the basilisk represented the pope, or head of the church, because of the crown on its head.

Bestiaries were richly illustrated. Since most Europeans could not read during the Middle Ages, monks hoped the pictures of animals would remind people of the lessons they had learned in church. As time went on, images of basilisks appeared in other places, too. The creatures were carved in stone, used as decorations on furniture, painted on walls, made into mosaics, and woven into tapestries.

No matter how familiar images of basilisks became, however, people were still afraid of them. Nobody knew where they might hide or when they would strike. While people had different ideas about how basilisks looked, everyone agreed they did not want to be a victim of one.

Chapter 2

The Legendary Basilisk

According to legend, basilisks were the deadliest creatures on Earth. In spite of their lethal reputation, however, the size of basilisks did not grow over the centuries as the stories of their powers increased. Legendary basilisks remained about 2 feet (0.6m) long, the same size as ordinary snakes.

In one way, this made the basilisk a deadlier monster. If basilisks were huge, thundering creatures, people would see and hear them long before they were close enough to attack. Instead, mythical basilisks were small enough to hide almost anywhere. People never knew when they might encounter them. They could be the victims of a basilisk attack at any time, and in any place.

Rocky Horror

One legend tells of an Italian **nobleman** who became the unsuspecting victim of a basilisk attack while he was hunting with his dog. In medieval times, hunting was a festive event where noblemen

An ancient Greek text depicts the serpent-like basilisk with horns.

showed off their skills with bows and arrows, spears, and clubs. Their favorite prey was deer. Hunting not only provided meat to eat, but it also trained men for war.

During this legendary hunt, the nobleman's dog left its master and began barking at a pile of rocks. The nobleman followed the dog to find out why it was so excited. When he did so, a fierce winged serpent confronted him in the rocks.

As the nobleman scrambled for his weapons, the serpent spread its wings and opened its mouth. A cloud of poisonous breath blew into the nobleman's face. Overcome by the poison, the nobleman collapsed on the ground. When his friends found him, he lived just long enough to tell them about the attack of the deadly basilisk.

The Baker's Curse

In the 13th century, a bakery in Vienna became the scene of another basilisk encounter. One night an angry crowd gathered outside the bakery and demanded that the baker be arrested. Before the crowd broke the door down, guards rushed in, followed by the master of justice. The master of justice commanded the baker to explain why the townspeople were rioting at his door.

The baker explained that the crowd was upset because there was a basilisk in his well. He added that this was not his fault and that he had done nothing wrong. The crowd, however, insisted there would be no basilisk if the baker had not conjured the monster to life with his careless words.

The trouble started, the baker said, when his new **apprentice**, Hans, asked to marry his daughter, Apollonia. The baker did not think anyone was good enough to marry her—least of all an apprentice. The baker became so angry he chased the apprentice out the door, cursing. Then, just as his rooster crowed, the baker bellowed that the apprentice could marry his daughter when his rooster laid an egg. This, the townspeople believed, had brought the basilisk to life.

The Fear Spreads

One month later the baker asked a maidservant to fetch water. When she noticed a ghastly smell coming from the well, she ran and told the baker. The baker sent his apprentice to investigate. The smell was so disgusting, that Hans nearly choked as he disappeared down into the well.

Suddenly, the apprentice let out a terrible cry. When the baker pulled him up, Hans was unconscious. Waking up several minutes later, he said he had seen a terrible monster with the head of a rooster and the body of a serpent. Its eyes blazed like fire and a crown glistened on its head. News of the basilisk spread, and soon the entire town was in an uproar.

This basilisk statue on a fountain in Switzerland presents no trouble compared to the legendary basilisk lurking in one of Vienna's wells.

The Legendary Basilisk

The basilisk with its rooster head and serpent tail presented villagers with a horrifying sight.

When the master of justice heard the baker's story, he ordered the guards to bring forth the wisest man in Vienna. The guards searched from house to house until they found a **scholar**. The scholar said that the only way to get rid of the monster was with a mirror. The basilisk was so hideous it would die of fright as soon as it saw itself. But if the person carrying the mirror did not move quickly, the scholar warned, he or she would be killed before the monster saw its reflection.

The master of justice turned to the townspeople and asked for a volunteer to attempt this feat. Immediately, someone from the back of the crowd shouted that he would go. It was Hans. The master of justice decreed that if Hans slayed the basilisk, he could marry the baker's daughter.

According to legend, a basilisk that sees its own reflection will die instantly.

Armed with only a mirror, Hans slowly climbed the rope back down into the well. As soon as the basilisk saw its terrifying reflection, it burst apart and turned into pieces of stone. After the townspeople celebrated the wedding of Hans and Apollonia, they carved a plaque on a slab of stone and mounted it outside the bakery so everyone would remember the young apprentice and how he defeated the deadly basilisk. The plaque can still be seen in Vienna today.

Basilisk Plague

Basilisk stories did not always tell of a single basilisk. According to legend, Ireland once suffered a plague of basilisks. To destroy the monsters, a brave man put on a suit of mirrors and walked from one end of the country to the other. Every basilisk that saw its reflection in the mirrors died instantly. Some legends say this brave man was Saint Patrick.

Saint Patrick was born on the west coast of Britain at the end of the 4th century. As an adult, he journeyed to Ireland as a Christian missionary. He traveled through the Irish countryside for 30 years teaching the people and building churches. Because Saint Patrick was a missionary, many believe that the stories of the basilisk plague were symbolic instead of true to life. Basilisks symbolized the **pagan** beliefs of the people, who did not believe in the God of the Bible. The brave man in

Basilisks

Saint Patrick preached throughout Ireland during the country's basilisk plague.

The Legendary Basilisk

the story who rid Ireland of basilisks represented Saint Patrick, who traveled through Ireland ridding the people of pagan beliefs.

Cellar Surprise

One of the last recorded basilisk attacks occurred in 1587 in Warsaw, Poland. One day, two five-year-old girls were playing hide-and-seek in an old abandoned cellar. When they scrambled down to the bottom of the stairs, the children collapsed and died.

Their mothers did not realize they were gone until it was dark. When the children did not answer their calls, they sent a servant to find them. After a while, the servant discovered the children at the bottom of the stairs in the abandoned cellar. Thinking they were only asleep, the servant descended the stairs. She too collapsed and died.

Soon, a curious neighbor who watched the servant disappear into the abandoned cellar followed. She found the swollen and yellow bodies at the bottom of the stairs. Afraid for her own life, she ran out of the cellar and cried for help.

The townspeople gathered and retrieved the bodies. When the king's physician declared they had died from a basilisk attack, the people searched for a brave volunteer to kill the monster. But no one volunteered. Everyone was too afraid. So they decided that someone already **condemned** to death should do it. Thousands gathered as they dressed

Basilisks

this criminal in protective glasses and leather covered with mirrors and sent him into the cellar. After a long time, the man came out carrying what looked like a snake. The people cheered. He had captured the basilisk.

Scientists began to wonder if basilisks were more myth than reality in the 1500s, when this drawing was created.

Beginning of the End

By the 16th century, the legend of the basilisk began to fade. Natural scientists began questioning what was commonly accepted and replaced myth with their own educated opinions and observations. For example, between 1551 and 1558 Swiss naturalist Konrad Gesner wrote *History of Animals,* declaring that the basilisk monster was "women's gossip and false nonsense."[3] During the 17th century, an English physician named Sir Thomas Brown studied the traditional stories about animals such as centaurs, griffins, and basilisks. He decided that most of the tales were completely false and wrote his findings in a book that became known as *Vulgar Errors.*

Ultimately, however, the basilisk simply sank under the weight of its own fantastic powers. According to legend, anyone who looked upon a basilisk was instantly killed, so nobody should have been able to describe such a creature. Yet the legend of the basilisk did not completely disappear. Just as the basilisk's powers made it too fantastic to be real, they also made it unforgettable.

Chapter 3

The Basilisk Strikes Again

Today, basilisks are not merely the stuff of legend. Monsters based on the classic basilisk monster are an ever-growing presence in popular culture. They have slithered into children's literature, fantasy fiction books, and short stories. They are seen in comics, movies, and **role-playing games** such as Dungeons & Dragons and Final Fantasy. In department stores, basilisks are lined up on the shelves of the toy section. Just like that of the legendary basilisk, the basilisk's popularity in the 20th century grew little by little, story by story.

The basilisk, pictured here on the column of an old church in France, is part of popular culture today in comic books and movies.

Silent Horror

A basilisk appeared on the big screen for the first time in a 28-minute 1914 British silent horror picture called *The Basilisk*. Even though the basilisk's name is in the title, the creature does not appear on the screen very long. Instead, the movie focuses on an evil **hypnotist** who wants to cast a beautiful woman under his spell. All he has to do is make her kill her boyfriend, and then she will be his.

At the end, exactly as the hypnotist plans, the woman walks to her sleeping boyfriend with a dagger in her hand. She raises the dagger high into the air. Then, just as she is about to stab him, a gigantic basilisk attacks the evil hypnotist with a deadly bite. In an instant, the spell is broken and the woman and her boyfriend are saved.

This is probably the only time that a basilisk played the hero in a story instead of the villain. Unfortunately, it is impossible to see this movie any more. The movie was made so long ago that it has been lost.

Modern Marvel

In December 1973, the basilisk struck again—not in the movies, but in a comic book. The editors at Marvel Comics introduced a new villain—Basilisk—in the Marvel Team-up #16 issue, called *Beware of the Basilisk, My Son!*

In the comics, Basilisk does not start out as a powerful, villainous monster. Instead, he is a common criminal named Basil Elks. He has thinning hair and a mustache. One day while he is in prison, an inmate mocks him by calling him "Basilisk," after the mythical monster. The cruel name sticks, and soon Elks is scorned by all of the prisoners. The nickname not only makes fun of Elks's name, but it also highlights how weak and powerless he is compared to the legendary monster.

When Elks is released from prison, he decides to steal a magnificent emerald from a museum in New York City. Slowly and steadily, he creeps through the museum with his flashlight until he finds the glass case. The emerald inside glows. Elks opens the case and grabs the stone.

Before he can get away, a security guard orders him to stop. In that moment, Elks relives all the scorn he felt while he was in prison. Deciding that he will never go back to prison again, Elks grabs his gun. The security guard fires. Instead of hitting Elks, however, the security guard shoots the emerald, which is really a powerful Alpha-Stone that was once stolen from the alien Kree. As soon as the bullet smashes into the gem, the Alpha-Stone explodes.

Basil Elks's Powers

When the smoke clears, Elks has changed. His hair is gone and his clothes hang in shreds. He looks at the guard with large, fiery eyes. His skin has become green and thick like a lizard's, and his muscles bulge with superhuman strength.

At first, Elks does not realize how much he has changed. Thinking he must get away, he orders the guard to freeze. To Elks's surprise, a red ray blazes from his eyes, freezing the security guard like a giant ice cube.

Just like the legendary basilisk, Elks has become a powerful monster with a deadly stare. His eyes can shoot microwave beams that rearrange an object's **molecules**. If he makes the molecules speed up, he can generate heat up to 3,000°F (1,648°C). If

Basilisks

he slows molecules down, he can freeze objects under a sheet of ice. The force generated from his eyes can also blast him through the air like a rocket.

After obtaining another Kree stone, the Omega-Stone, Basilisk becomes strong enough to destroy civilization in revenge for all the scorn he has suffered. Using his powerful stare, he makes a chain of volcanoes begin to erupt, burying the world under

Spider-Man battled Marvel Comics' new villain, Basilisk, in 1973.

The Basilisk Strikes Again

molten lava. Basilisk's plan is thwarted when Spider-Man and the Thing knock him into one of his own volcanoes.

The story of the villainous Basilisk unfolds over numerous issues in which he battles Spider-Man, the Thing, and the Kree Captain Mar-Vell. Just like the basilisk monster, however, Basilisk can be defeated. After escaping from an underground prison, Basilisk finally meets his match in the Fantastic Four issue #289. Basilisk is shot and killed by the vigilante Scourge of the Underworld.

Let the Games Begin

A year after Marvel Comics introduced the villainous Basilisk, the basilisk raised its head again in the

In the role-playing video game Final Fantasy, a character will encounter basilisks on her quest.

first role-playing game, Dungeons & Dragons. In this game, players study a thick handbook and roll multishaped dice to become make-believe characters such as elves, dwarfs, humans, and halflings. Then one player, the Dungeon Master, becomes the storyteller. The Dungeon Master controls the story setting, secret maps, and other characters the players encounter on their quests. As players win battles, gather treasures, and earn points, they advance to higher levels.

Players battle many different types of creatures and monsters, including basilisks and their cousins, the cockatrices. Most of the time, basilisks guard treasure. Their dangerous claws, poisonous breath, and petrifying stare make them challenging monsters to defeat. Cockatrices attack anything that comes too close to their lair, turning the intruder's flesh into stone.

Basilisks became even more popular when role-playing games hit the video game system market. One game, Final Fantasy, was introduced in 1987 and became one of the most popular role-playing games ever made. In this game, players take on the role of the main character. Each game has different main characters and different quests to complete. Quests usually involve rebelling against a political power or destroying an enemy that is trying to take over the world. The main character meets many friends and foes throughout the game, including basilisks and cockatrices. Basilisks are usually

The Basilisk Strikes Again

green, dragonlike creatures that petrify unsuspecting travelers. Cockatrices look more like the traditional basilisk and turn opponents into stone.

Hot off the Press

The biggest boost to the basilisk's popularity came from J.K. Rowling's *Harry Potter and the Chamber of Secrets,* the second in a series of books about a young wizard named Harry Potter. Throughout her books, Rowling fills Harry's enchanted world with references to history and legend along with ideas from her own extraordinary imagination. In *Chamber,* Rowling gives a deadly basilisk a starring role and expands the familiar legend by inventing a character named Herpo the Foul, who bred the first basilisk. It is a particularly fitting name since it is based on the Greek word *herpein,* meaning "to creep," which is also the origin of the word "serpent."

Rowling reveals the basilisk's villainous identity little by little, chapter by chapter. When Harry and his friends uncover an important passage from an old library book, they realize they are facing a dangerous creature with monstrous powers. "Of the many fearsome beasts and monsters that roam our land," they read, "there is none more curious or more deadly than the Basilisk."[4]

Rowling's basilisk monster is a fascinating blend of new and traditional characteristics. Instead of being small, the basilisk is a gigantic creature. Yet just like the mythical monster, it was hatched from

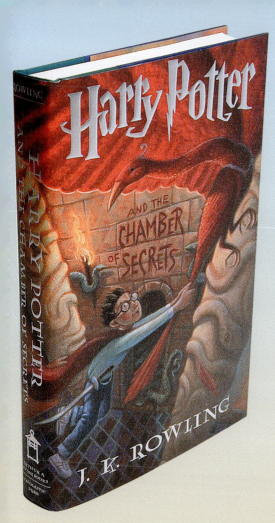

A gigantic basilisk becomes a dangerous foe for Harry Potter in the second book of J.K. Rowling's series.

an egg, and its stare kills all living things. By putting the basilisk under the power of the evil Lord Voldemort, Rowling created an extremely deadly foe for Harry and his friends at Hogwarts to defeat.

In 2002 *Harry Potter and the Chamber of Secrets* reached the big screen. Teams of 130 experts worked for months to bring the story to life for movie audiences around the world. One of the most challenging scenes to create was one in which Harry Potter faces the gigantic basilisk. Everyone

The Basilisk Strikes Again

Harry faces an 80-foot basilisk in the film version of Harry Potter and the Chamber of Secrets.

agreed that the 80-foot (24.4m) basilisk had to look real as it slithered through its watery underground chamber. To help create this basilisk monster, the team brought in a live 8-foot (2.4m) Burmese python named Doris as a model. Then the team concentrated on the water effects. They believed that if the water in the chamber did not look real, the monster would not look real either. The team decided to combine shots of actual water with computer-generated water. When the movie was finished, audiences held their breath as they

Basilisks

watched Harry battle the basilisk in 45 heart-pounding shots.

From literature and comics to the big screen, basilisks are a fascinating part of popular culture. Modern-day sightings of the basilisk include roaring electronic monsters on toy shelves, fantasy books such as *Basilisk* by N.M. Browne and *Song of the Basilisk* by Patricia A. McKillip, and evil monsters in role-playing games.

But the basilisk's current popularity should come as no surprise. Even though the legendary basilisk has changed over the centuries, people have not. People will always want to hear about monsters, including one of the deadliest creatures on Earth—the basilisk.

Notes

Chapter 1: Attack of the Basilisk
1. Quoted in Jerry Dennis, "Pliny's World: All the Facts–and Then Some," *Smithsonian,* November 1995, p. 152.
2. Quoted in Daniel Cohen, *A Modern Look at Monsters.* New York: Dodd, Mead, 1970, p. 21.

Chapter 2: The Legendary Basilisk
3. Quoted in Cohen, *A Modern Look at Monsters,* p. 22.

Chapter 3: The Basilisk Strikes Again
4. J.K. Rowling, *Harry Potter and the Chamber of Secrets.* New York: Arthur A. Levine, 1999, p. 290.

Glossary

apprentice: A person learning an art or trade from a skilled worker.

bestiaries: Medieval collections of animal stories that taught morals and lessons.

condemned: Found guilty of a crime and sentenced to death.

convulsions: Involuntary muscle contractions.

hypnotist: Someone who puts people in a sleep-like state, making them open to suggestion.

Jenny Hanivers: Fake monsters made and sold by sailors beginning in the 13th century.

landlubbers: People who know nothing about the sea or sailing.

medieval: Belonging to the Middle Ages.

Middle Ages: The period in western European history from the 5th century to the 15th century.

molecules: Two or more atoms held together by chemical forces.

mythical: Not real; existing only in the imagination.

nobleman: A man of noble rank; in medieval times, a man who was given land in return for defending a ruler or monarch.

pagan: A person who does not accept the God of the *Bible*.

petrified: Turned into stone or something hard like stone.

role-playing games: Games in which players take on the roles of characters in fantasy adventures.

scholar: A learned person.

For Further Exploration

Books

Laura Buller, *Myths and Monsters from Dragons to Werewolves*. London: Dorling Kindersley, 2003. Packed with fascinating facts about all sorts of creatures, including dragons, tricksters, serpents, and scary fairies.

Katie Edwards, *Myths and Monsters: Secrets Revealed*. Watertown, MA: Charlesbridge, 2004. Explores the origin of many mythological creatures, including dragons, mermaids, and sea serpents, and how they are connected with real creatures.

John Harris, *Greece! Rome! Monsters!* Los Angeles: Getty Trust Publications, 2002. Updated retelling of stories about twenty monsters from Greek and Roman mythology, such as centaurs, minotaurs, sirens, and basilisks. Includes a guide and pop quiz.

Web Sites

Harry Potter Movies (www.harrypotter.warner bros.com). This site features images and information on the latest Harry Potter movie, with links to a newsletter and message boards.

Interactive King Cobra, National Geographic (www.nationalgeographic.com/king cobra/index-n.html). Invites visitors on a journey to explore the habitat, diet, enemies, and myths and legends of the king cobra.

J.K. Rowling (www.jkrowling.com). The official Web site of author J.K. Rowling. In addition to an author biography and diary entries, the site discusses frequently asked questions, rumors, and daily news about the Harry Potter series.

Marvel Universe (www.marvel.com). The official Web site for Marvel comics features the latest information on Marvel superheroes in TV, movies, and comics.

Index

Apollonia (legendary character), 24

Basil Elks (comic book character), 31–34
Basilisk (Browne), 39
Basilisk, The (film), 30–31
bestiaries, 15–16
Beware of the Basilisk, My Son! (comic book), 31–34
birth, 5–6
books
 ancient, 13
 medieval, 15–16, 28
 recent, 4, 36–37, 39
books of beasts, 15–16
Brown, Sir Thomas, 28

Browne, N.M., 39

Captain Mar-Vell (comic book character), 34
cobras, 10–11
cockatrices, 35, 36
comic books, 31–34
descriptions, 4, 6, 36
devil, 15–16
Doris (Burmese python), 38
Dungeons and Dragons, 35

eggs, 5–6
encounters, 18–20, 22–24, 26–27
eyes, 7, 32–33

fake monsters, 13–15

Fantastic Four #289 (comic book), 34
Final Fantasy (video game), 35–36
French legends, 7

Gesner, Konrad, 28
Greeks, ancient, 8, 10

Hans (legendary character), 23–24
Harry Potter and the Chamber of Secrets (film), 37–39
Harry Potter and the Chamber of Secrets (Rowling), 4, 36–37
hatchlings, 6
Herpo the Foul (fictional character), 36
Historia Naturalis (Pliny the Elder), 13
history, 5
History of Animals (Gesner), 28

Irish legend, 24, 26
Italian legend, 18–19

Jenny Hanivers, 13–14

killing methods, 7–8, 11
king cobras, 10–11

legs, 7

Marvel Comics, 31–34
McKillip, Patricia A., 39
Middle Ages
 books written during, 15–16, 28
 legends during, 18–20, 22–24, 26–27
mirrors, 8, 22–24, 27
mongoose, 11
monks, 15–16
movies, 30–31, 37–39

name, 8, 10

odor, 20

pagans, 24, 26
Patrick, Saint, 24, 26

Basilisks

plague, 24, 26
Pliny the Elder, 12–13
poison, 7
powers
 in comic books, 32–34
 in legends, 7, 11

role-playing games, 35
Romans, ancient, 8, 10, 12–13
roosters, 5–6, 8
Rowling, J. K., 4, 36

size, 17
snakes, 10–11, 15–16, 38

Song of the Basilisk (McKillip), 39
Spider-Man (comic book character), 34

Thing, the (comic book character), 34
toys, 29

video games, 35–36
Viennese legend, 19–20, 22–24
Vulgar Errors (Brown), 28

Warsaw (Poland), 26–27
weasels, 7–8, 11

About the Author

Lori Mortensen is the author of more than 100 stories and articles for children which have appeared in magazines such as *Highlights for Children, Ladybug, Wild Outdoor World,* and many others. When she is not writing, she enjoys spending time with her husband, three children, three cats, and her son's slithering ball python. This is her first book.